crêpes

crêpes

whitecap

Published in Canada and the United States in 2007 by Whitecap Books Ltd. For more information, please contact Whitecap Books Ltd., 351 Lynn Avenue, North Vancouver, British Columbia, Canada V7J 2C4.

Visit our website at www.whitecap.ca.

First published in 2002 by Hamlyn, a division of Octopus Publishing Group Ltd, 2–4 Heron Quays, London E14 4JP

ISBN-13: 978-1-55285-839-4
ISBN-10: 1-55285-839-1

Printed and bound in China by Toppan

10 9 8 7 6 5 4 3 2 1

Photographer: Gus Filgate
Food Stylist: Joanna Farrow

Notes

1 The American Egg Board advises that eggs should not be consumed raw. This book contains some dishes made with raw or lightly cooked eggs. It is prudent for more vulnerable people such as pregnant and nursing mothers, invalids, the elderly, babies, and young children to avoid uncooked or lightly cooked dishes made with eggs.

2 Meat and poultry should be cooked thoroughly. To test if poultry is cooked, pierce the flesh through the thickest part with a skewer or fork–the juices should run clear, never pink or red. Keep refrigerated until ready for cooking.

3 This book includes dishes made with nuts and nut derivatives. It is advisable for those with known allergic reactions to nuts and nut derivatives and those who may potentially be vulnerable to these allergies, such as pregnant and nursing mothers, invalids, the elderly, babies, and children, to avoid dishes made with nuts and nut oils. It is also prudent to check the labels of pre-prepared ingredients for the possible inclusion of nut derivatives.

4 Exercise caution when working with hot or flaming alcohol, especially if cooking near draperies or other flammable materials. Do not add more alcohol than the recipe states, and do not pour extra liqueur from the bottle into a pan of flaming liqueur. Have a fire extinguisher or damp towels at hand.

contents

introduction

Delicious and simple to make from ingredients in the pantry, crêpes—in one form or another—have been sautéed, rolled around all kinds of fillings, or served plain in many countries throughout the world for centuries. But it was, perhaps inevitably, France that raised this modest little dish to greater culinary heights. Although now best known as a dessert, crêpes (the French word for pancakes) were traditionally served as an appetizer. They were filled with ham, cheese, mushrooms or shellfish, often coated in a creamy sauce. In the course of time, different regions of France began to produce their own specialties and both Brittany and Agen lay claim to first serving them at the end, rather than at the beginning of a meal.

Throughout the Christian world, they are traditionally cooked on Mardi Gras, the day before the Lenten fast begins. It has often been suggested that this close association resulted from frugal housewives using up their stocks of eggs and butter before they were banned for the next forty days and, undoubtedly, there is an element of truth in this.

However, the symbolism of crêpes is much greater than mere practicality and each of the ingredients bears a special significance. Flour is the staff of life, eggs represent creation, milk symbolizes purity, and salt is a sign of wholesomeness. Many French families still carry out the traditional custom of making a wish, while touching the handle of the pan with one hand, holding a coin and turning the crêpe with the other. In England, pancake races and other games are relics of a more riotous celebration. European Catholics also serve crêpes on Candlemas Day—2 February—as a symbol of renewal and hope.

Of course, despite being associated with certain festivals, crêpes are eaten and enjoyed throughout the year. Crêperies have spread from their native Brittany to Germany, Austria, Britain, and the United States. One restaurant in the Belgian city of Bruges even claims to serve the biggest selection of crêpes in the world. For the home cook, they are the perfect solution to the perennial question of what to serve for the family's supper. Always popular, they can provide a quick, substantial, and inexpensive main course, filled with bacon, chicken, shrimp, spinach, cheese, or mushrooms, or a delicious dessert treat, sprinkled with sugar and lemon juice, smothered in syrup, filled with fruit, or flavored with chocolate. They may even be cut into thin strips and used to garnish soup, or stacked, layered with cream, jam, or fruit, to make a cake.

Choosing a pan

As with any task, using the right equipment makes it much easier to make crêpes. It is possible to cook crêpes in a standard skillet, but they risk being uneven, may stick, are more difficult to turn, and so are more likely to break up. Using a special crêpe pan, which is smaller and has a smooth base and gently sloping curved sides, virtually guarantees success. The most popular size is 7–8 inches, but you can also buy pans as large as 10 inches. Note that these measurements refer to the diameter of the rim of the pan and not to the size of the crêpe itself. Pans may be made of a variety of materials, but it is important that they are heavy so that the batter cooks quickly and evenly. Buy a sturdy pan that will last a long time. Keep your pan exclusively for cooking crêpes; if you use it to cook other foods, you may spoil the essential smoothness of the base. Always follow the manufacturer's instructions for cleaning the pan after use; these will vary depending on the metal used and on whether it has a nonstick lining.

Traditional pans were made of cast iron and some cooks maintain that these are still the best for crêpes made with buckwheat flour. They take quite a long time to heat up, but distribute the heat very evenly. You will need to season a

new cast-iron pan. Sprinkle a layer of salt over the base and heat gently. Tip out the excess salt and rub the pan with a little vegetable oil, using paper towels. Be careful not to burn your hand. Leave the pan slightly oily before using it for the first time. If the pan is well seasoned, you will need very little oil for cooking crêpes. If possible, do not wash the pan after use; simply wipe it clean with paper towels. If you later need to season it again, wash it thoroughly in hot water and detergent, dry it well, and repeat the process.

Heavy-gauge steel pans are also available, although they are more often labeled omelet, rather than crêpe pans. Nevertheless, they are still the same shape with a flat base and sloping sides. These pans need careful seasoning with vegetable oil alone. Like cast-iron pans, they should not be washed, but simply wiped clean with paper towels and then oiled again before storage to prevent rusting.

While seasoning a cast-iron or steel pan effectively makes it nonstick, many people prefer to play safe and use a more modern pan with a synthetic resin coating, such as Teflon, or a hard-anodized lining. These pans are usually made of heavy-gauge aluminum and the nonstick lining is very smooth and durable. Use wooden spatulas and tools to avoid scratching the surface and never clean them with anything abrasive. When buying a pan, it is always worth checking the firmness of the

handle. If it is not securely welded or riveted, you not only risk ruining your crêpes, but also burning yourself. Some pans are cast in one piece with their handles and, while these are very secure, the handles are likely to become quite hot.

Tabletop, electric, nonstick crêpe pans are also available, but these are more suitable for use in restaurants than at home—unless you are addicted to Crêpes Suzette and other flambéed crêpes. Most have a flat pan in which the batter is cooked in the conventional way, but some have a convex base, which is first dipped in the batter and then reversed for cooking.

Ingredients

A basic crêpe batter consists of all-purpose flour, salt, egg, and milk. Buckwheat flour may be substituted for half the wheat flour. Some cooks prefer to use a mixture of equal parts of milk and water, rather than milk alone— water makes the crêpes very light, milk makes the batter smooth, and helps the crêpes turn golden. Using half beer and half milk will cause the crêpes to rise slightly and gives them a savory flavor. Light chicken stock may also be included. For a richer batter, you can add an extra egg to the basic recipe, but reduce the milk by 2 tablespoons.

Batter for dessert crêpes can also include a little superfine or vanilla sugar

to sweeten it. Individual recipes may specify additional ingredients. Semisweet chocolate can be melted in the milk, for example, or a spoonful of brandy or liqueur can be whisked into it for extra flavoring. Finely grated citrus rind, orange or lemon juice, orange flower water, ground cinnamon, apple pie spice, and almond or vanilla extract are popular additions.

Stirring 1–2 tablespoons of melted butter or bland-tasting vegetable oil, such as peanut or safflower, into the batter just before cooking the crêpes gives them a rich flavor and also helps to prevent them from sticking to the pan. Always use sweet butter for dessert crêpes.

Batters may also be made with yeast, although these are more often used for coatings than for crêpes. Russian blinis are the best-known example of a yeast-based batter, but are less familiar than the rolled or folded crêpe. Light and airy, they are small and usually served with a topping, frequently smoked salmon or caviar and sour cream.

Crêpes may be sautéed in oil or melted butter. Traditionally, in France, butter is used for the flavor and the rich golden color it gives to the crêpes. It is best to use a bland vegetable oil or sweet butter for best results. If the pan is a nonstick one or it has been properly seasoned, it will probably require no more than an occasional brushing with oil or butter, depending on how many crêpes you are cooking at the time.

How to make the perfect crêpe

The basic crêpe batter can be used for both savory and sweet dishes and the technique remains the same when making flavored batters. The secret of success is to avoid over-beating. Beat the ingredients only until they are combined and smooth. Too much whisking causes the gluten in the flour to develop and, as a result, the crêpes will be tough and chewy. The exception is when making yeast batter, which requires vigorous beating to develop the gluten. You may need to adjust the quantity of liquid you add to the batter, as individual flours vary. Aim for a fairly thin, pourable consistency.

It is not essential to let the batter rest, but it does produce a lighter result. Crêpes made from freshly prepared batter tend to have a bubbly, rather than a flat surface. Pour the batter into a pitcher, cover, and set aside in a cool place for about 30 minutes to let the starch in the flour swell. When you are ready to cook the crêpes, if the batter has begun to separate, stir well to remix, but do not overmix. If the batter has been standing for a longer period, it may have thickened and you will need to stir in a little more liquid. Do not leave the batter to stand for more than 12 hours or it will begin to ferment.

As each crêpe is cooked, slide it out of the pan onto a flat plate. Stack the crêpes, interleaved with waxed paper or baking parchment to prevent them sticking, and keep warm over a pan of gently simmering water or in a very low oven. Alternatively, you can allow the crêpes to cool—still stacked and interleaved—then wrap carefully in foil and store in the refrigerator or freezer. Cook the remaining crêpes in the same way, brushing the pan with more oil or melted butter, if required.

Storing crêpes

If the crêpes are to be used right away, simply stack them on a plate and keep them warm. If you are making them ahead to use later in the day or to store overnight in the refrigerator, interleave them with squares of parchment paper to keep them from sticking together. To freeze crêpes, interleave with parchment paper and wrap in foil. They can be frozen for up to 3 months. They will also keep in the refrigerator, wrapped in the same way, for up to two days. To serve, thaw overnight in the refrigerator, if frozen, then reheat in a pan over low heat or in a low oven.

Filling and serving

Unlike omelets, most crêpes are not filled while still in the pan. There are a few exceptions, such as egg and cheese crêpes, when an egg is cracked on top of the just cooked crêpe and then sprinkled with cheese once it has set, before the crêpe is folded and tipped out of the pan. More usually, the filling is simply spooned into the crêpe, which is then rolled or folded. After folding, savory crêpes may be covered with a sauce, sprinkled with grated cheese, and briefly baked in the oven. These are popular folds for sweet or savory crêpes:

The basic roll Lay the crêpe on a plate or work surface and spoon some filling in a ribbon down the center. Fold one side of the crêpe over the filling to cover it, then the other side over the first to form a neat roll with the filling showing at both ends.

The cigarette Lay the crêpe down and spread the filling thinly over the whole of it. Starting at one edge, roll the crêpe into a long, thin cylinder.

The parcel Lay the crêpe down and place a spoonful of filling in the center of it. Fold both sides over the filling, then fold the bottom edge over it. Finally, fold the top edge down to make a neat parcel. Turn over and serve.

The baton Lay the crêpe down and spoon some filling into the centre of it. Fold over both sides to cover the filling, then roll up the crêpe from the bottom to form a neat roll.

The triangle Fold the crêpe in half and in half again to form a triangle. Stuff one of the pockets with filling and serve.

The stack Lay a crêpe on a serving plate and spread some filling over the top. Lay another crêpe on top, then top with more filling. Continue until all the filling and all the crêpes have been used.

basic crêpes

1¼ cups all-purpose flour

a pinch of salt

1 egg, lightly beaten

1¼ cups milk

light olive oil, vegetable oil or butter, for greasing pan

These plain crêpes can be used for any savory crêpe recipe, or for dessert recipes when you don't want too sweet or rich a flavor.

1 Put the flour and salt in a bowl and make a well in the center. Pour the egg and some of the milk into the well. Whisk the liquid, gradually incorporating the flour to make a smooth paste. Whisk in the remaining milk, then pour the batter into a measuring cup with a pouring spout. Allow to rest, if desired.

2 Put a little oil or butter into a 7-inch crêpe pan or heavy-based skillet and heat until it starts to smoke. Pour off the excess and pour a little batter into the pan, tilting it until the base is coated with a thin layer. (Or, if you prefer, use a small ladle to measure the batter into the pan.) Cook for 1–2 minutes until the underside begins to turn golden.

3 Flip the crêpe with an offset spatula and cook for a further 30–45 seconds until it is golden on the second side. Slide the crêpe out of the pan and make the remaining crêpes, greasing the pan as necessary.

Makes 8–10 crêpes
Preparation time: **5 minutes, plus resting (optional)**
Cooking time: **15–25 minutes**

variations

spinach crêpes

Trim the stalks from half a pound of washed spinach leaves and put the leaves in a heavy-based saucepan. Cover the pan with a lid and cook the spinach for 2 minutes or until wilted. Drain thoroughly, pressing out any excess water. Chop finely and beat into the batter with the milk.

herb crêpes

Finely chop a small handful of fresh herbs such as parsley, basil, tarragon, dill, chervil, or oregano. Beat into the batter.

whole-wheat crêpes

Replace the white flour with whole-wheat flour, or, for a lighter alternative, use half whole-wheat and half white flour.

buckwheat crêpes

1¼ cups buckwheat flour

a pinch of salt

3 eggs, lightly beaten

1¼ cups milk

light olive oil, vegetable oil or butter, for greasing pan

These have a richer, nuttier flavor than crêpes made with white flour and are delicious in both sweet and savory recipes. Buckwheat flour is widely available in supermarkets and health food stores.

1 Put the flour and salt in a bowl and make a well in the center. Add the eggs and some of the milk and whisk together, gradually incorporating the flour. Add the remaining milk and mix to a smooth paste. Pour into a measuring cup with a spout. Allow to rest, if desired.

2 Put a little oil or butter in a 7-inch crêpe pan or heavy-based skillet and heat until it starts to smoke. Pour off the excess and pour a little batter into the pan, tilting it until the base is coated in a thin layer. (Or, if you prefer, use a small ladle to measure the batter into the pan.) Cook for 1–2 minutes until the underside begins to turn golden.

3 Flip the crêpe with an offset spatula and cook for a further 30–45 seconds until golden on the second side. Slide the crêpe out of the pan and make the remaining crêpes, greasing the pan as necessary.

Makes 8–10 crêpes
Preparation time: **5 minutes, plus resting (optional)**
Cooking time: **15–25 minutes**

sweet crêpes

1¼ cups all-purpose flour

a pinch of salt

¼ cup superfine sugar

1 egg, lightly beaten

1¼ cups milk

2 tablespoons sweet butter, melted

light olive oil, vegetable oil or butter, for greasing pan

1 Put the flour, salt, and sugar in a bowl and make a well in the center. Pour the egg and some of the milk into the well. Whisk the liquid, gradually incorporating the flour to make a smooth paste. Whisk in the butter, then the remaining milk until smooth. Pour the batter into a measuring cup with a pouring spout. Allow to rest, if liked.

2 Put a little oil or butter in a 7-inch crêpe pan or heavy-based skillet and heat until it starts to smoke. Pour off the excess and pour a little batter into the pan, tilting it until the base is coated in a thin layer. (Or, if you prefer, use a small ladle to measure the batter into the pan.) Cook for 1–2 minutes until the underside begins to turn golden.

3 Flip the crêpe with an offset spatula and cook for a further 30–45 seconds until golden on the second side. Slide the crêpe out of the pan and make the remaining crêpes, greasing the pan as necessary.

Makes 8–10 crêpes
Preparation time: **5 minutes, plus resting (optional)**
Cooking time: **15–25 minutes**

lemon and cinnamon crêpes

1 tablespoon butter

1¼ cups all-purpose flour

½ teaspoon ground cinnamon

a pinch of salt

1 teaspoon grated lemon zest

1 egg, beaten

1¼ cups milk

oil or butter, for greasing pan

To serve:

sugar

lemon wedges

1 Melt the butter in a small pan. Sift the flour, cinnamon, salt, and grated lemon zest into a bowl, make a well in the center and gradually beat in the egg, milk, and melted butter to make a smooth batter.

2 Put a little oil or butter in a 7-inch crêpe pan or heavy-based skillet and heat until it starts to smoke. Pour off the excess and pour a little batter into the pan, tilting it until the base is coated in a thin layer. (Or, if you prefer, use a small ladle to measure the batter into the pan.) Cook for 1–2 minutes until the underside begins to turn golden.

3 Flip the crêpe with an offset spatula and cook for a further 30–45 seconds until golden on the second side. Slide the crêpe out of the pan and make the remaining crêpes, greasing the pan as necessary.

4 Serve 2–3 crêpes per person, dusted with sugar and accompanied with lemon wedges.

Makes 8 crêpes
Preparation time: **5 minutes**
Cooking time: **15–25 minutes**

whole-wheat honey crêpes

1 cup whole-wheat self-rising flour

1 egg, beaten

1¼ cups milk

½ cup liquid honey

½ cup raisins

a pinch of grated nutmeg

1 Put the flour in a bowl and make a well in the center. Pour in the egg and milk and beat to a smooth batter. In another bowl, mix together the honey, raisins, and nutmeg.

2 Using a lightly greased crêpe pan and the batter, cook 8 crêpes (*see page* 12) and keep them warm. Spread each crêpe with a spoonful of the honey mixture, and then fold to form a wedge-shaped parcel. Serve immediately.

Makes 8 crêpes
Preparation time: **5–10 minutes**
Cooking time: **15–25 minutes**

chocolate crêpes

1 cup all-purpose flour

2 tablespoons cocoa powder

¼ cup superfine sugar

1 egg

1¼ cups milk

oil or butter, for greasing pan

1 Sift the flour and cocoa powder into a bowl, then stir in the sugar. Add the egg and a little milk, and whisk to make a stiff batter. Beat in the remaining milk.

2 Put a little oil or butter in a 7-inch crêpe pan or heavy-based skillet and heat until it starts to smoke. Pour off the excess and pour a little batter into the pan, tilting it until the base is coated in a thin layer. (Or, if you prefer, use a small ladle to measure the batter into the pan.) Cook for 1–2 minutes until the underside begins to turn golden.

3 Flip the crêpe with an offset spatula and cook for a further 30–45 seconds until golden on the second side. Slide the crêpe out of the pan and make the remaining crêpes, greasing the pan as necessary.

Makes about 8 crêpes
Preparation time: **5–10 minutes**
Cooking time: **15–25 minutes**

zucchini crêpes with emmental cheese and pepper sauce

1 quantity Basic Crêpe batter
(*see page* 12)

2 tablespoons chopped thyme

3 cups grated zucchini

¾ cup olive oil

1 eggplant, about 10 ounces, cut
into small chunks

2 small red onions, sliced

2 red bell peppers, cored, seeded,
and sliced

1 x 14.5-ounce can chopped
tomatoes

¼ cup balsamic vinegar

10 ounces Emmental or Gruyère
cheese, thinly sliced

oil or butter, for greasing pan

salt and pepper

These crisp little crêpes, topped with melting cheese and a ratatouille-style topping, make a very good appetizer. Alternatively, you can make larger crêpes and serve them with a salad as an entrée.

1 Pour the crêpe batter into a large bowl and stir in the thyme and the grated zucchini. Season with salt and pepper. Set aside.

2 Heat the olive oil in a large heavy-based saucepan or skillet. Add the eggplant and onions and sauté for about 5 minutes until they start to turn golden. Add the peppers and continue to sauté quickly for 3 minutes until the vegetables are lightly browned. Add the tomatoes and vinegar and season with salt and pepper. Reduce the heat and simmer gently, uncovered, for 10 minutes while cooking the crêpes.

3 Heat a little oil or butter in a large crêpe pan or griddle. Put about 2 tablespoons of the crêpe mixture on one side of the pan and spread to around 4 inches. Add as many more measures of batter as the pan will hold and fry for about 2 minutes or until golden on the underside. Flip the crêpes and cook for 2 minutes longer. Drain on paper towels and transfer to a baking tray. Cook the remainder of the crêpes (the mixture should make 12 in all).

4 Arrange the cheese slices over the crêpes and broil under a preheated broiler until the cheese is melting. Arrange 2 crêpes on each dessert plate, overlapping them slightly. Pile the pepper sauce on top and serve warm.

Serves 6
Preparation time: **10 minutes, plus making the crêpe batter**

spinach and ricotta crêpes

1 quantity Basic Crêpes (*see page* 12)

½ cup cooked spinach

1 egg, beaten

½ cup ricotta cheese

¼ cup grated Parmesan cheese

2 tablespoons butter

⅔ cup chicken stock

salt and pepper

1 Make the crêpes and set them aside while making the filling.

2 Chop the spinach. Stir in the egg, ricotta, and half of the Parmesan cheese. Season with salt and pepper. Divide the mixture among the crêpes, roll them up, and put them in a lightly greased, shallow baking dish. Dot with the butter and the remaining cheese and add the stock. Bake in a preheated oven at 400°F for 20 minutes. Serve immediately.

Makes about 8 crêpes
Preparation time: **10 minutes, plus crêpe-making time**
Cooking time: **20 minutes**

spinach crêpes with asparagus

24 thick asparagus spears, trimmed

8 Spinach Crêpes (*see page* 13)

vegetable oil, for greasing baking dish

Béchamel sauce:

1¼ cups milk

1 small onion, roughly chopped

1 bay leaf

2 tablespoons butter

¼ cup all-purpose flour

salt and pepper

½ cup mild white Cheddar cheese, grated

1 First make the béchamel sauce. Put the milk, onion, and bay leaf into a saucepan and heat until just boiling. Remove from the heat and set aside for 20 minutes to infuse. Strain the milk and reserve. Meanwhile make the crêpes and set them aside.

2 Melt the butter in a saucepan, stir in the flour, and cook over a low heat for 1 minute. Remove from the heat and beat in the infused milk, a little at a time, until blended. Return to a low heat and stir constantly until thickened. Bring to a gentle boil, stirring, then simmer for 2 minutes. Season with salt and pepper.

3 Blanch the asparagus spears in a large pan of lightly salted boiling water for 2 minutes. Drain, refresh under cold running water, and pat dry with a paper towel.

4 Place 3 asparagus spears on each crêpe and roll them up. Place the crêpes seam-side down in a lightly greased, shallow baking dish. Pour the béchamel sauce over them and sprinkle with the cheese.

5 Place the dish under a preheated broiler and cook for 8–10 minutes until bubbling and golden. Serve at once.

Serves 4
Preparation time: **10 minutes, plus crêpe-making time and infusing the milk**
Cooking time: **15–20 minutes**

savory florentine layer

8 Herb Crêpes (*see page* 13)

Tomato filling:

1 x 8-ounce can tomatoes

1 tablespoon butter

1 medium onion, chopped

2 garlic cloves, finely chopped

¾ cup grated Parmesan cheese,
plus more for sprinkling

2 tablespoons chopped oregano

salt and pepper

Spinach filling:

10 cups baby spinach leaves

2 tablespoons butter

2 tablespoons milk

2 tablespoons cornstarch

⅔ cup heavy cream

a pinch of grated nutmeg

In this recipe, in which crêpes are interleaved with alternate layers of creamy spinach and tomato fillings to form a succulent stack, they are transformed into an elegant dinner party dish.

1 Make the crêpes and keep them warm while making the fillings.

2 To make the tomato filling, purée the tomatoes in a food processor or blender or press them through a sieve. Melt the butter in a saucepan, add the onion, and cook gently until soft. Add the garlic and cook for 1 minute. Blend in the tomatoes and cook, stirring, until the mixture thickens. Add the cheese, oregano, and salt and pepper to taste then heat gently for 1 minute.

3 To make the spinach filling, wash the spinach and put it in a saucepan with the water that clings to the leaves. Add the butter, cover the pan, and cook gently until wilted. Blend the milk with the cornstarch and set aside. Add the cream to the spinach with the nutmeg and salt and pepper to taste. Bring to a boil and simmer for 2 minutes. Stir in the blended cornstarch and cook, stirring, until the mixture thickens.

4 To serve, layer the crêpes on a warm serving platter with alternating layers of the tomato and spinach fillings. Serve hot, sprinkled with Parmesan and cut into wedges.

Serves 4
Preparation time: **15 minutes, plus crêpe-making time**
Cooking time: **20 minutes**

caramelized onion and emmental cheese crêpes

⅓ **cup whole grain mustard**

1 quantity Whole-wheat Crêpe Batter (*see page* 13)

oil or butter, for greasing pan

Filling:

3 tablespoons butter

3 onions, thinly sliced

2 teaspoons superfine sugar

a few thyme sprigs

2 cups grated Emmental or Gruyère cheese

salt and pepper

1 Stir the mustard into the crêpe batter and cook the crêpes following the instructions on page 12. Set the crêpes aside while making the filling.

2 To make the filling, melt the butter in a heavy-based pan and sauté the onions with the sugar for about 8–10 minutes until they are a deep golden color and caramelized. Tear the thyme leaves off the stems and add them to the pan with salt and plenty of black pepper.

3 Set aside ¼ cup of the cheese and sprinkle the remainder over the crêpes. Scatter the sautéed onions over the cheese then roll up the crêpes and arrange them in a lightly greased, shallow baking dish. Sprinkle with the reserved cheese and bake in a preheated oven at 375°F for about 15 minutes until the cheese has melted. Serve warm.

Serves 4
Preparation time: **10 minutes, plus making the crêpe batter**
Cooking time: **about 40 minutes**

crêpes with wild mushrooms, sherry, and cream

⅔ cup dried porcini mushrooms

⅔ cup boiling water

1 quantity Basic Crêpes
(*see page* 12)

2 tablespoons butter

1 onion, chopped

2 garlic cloves, sliced

3 cups sliced cremini or
button mushrooms

2 tablespoons chopped thyme

⅓ cup chopped flat-leaf parsley

⅓ cup medium sherry

⅔ cup heavy or whipping cream

salt and pepper

spinach or other greens, to serve

The classic combination of mushrooms, sherry, and cream makes a lovely filling for crêpes and is quick and simple to prepare.

1 Put the dried mushrooms in a small bowl, cover with the boiling water and leave to soak for 15 minutes. Meanwhile, make the crêpes and set them aside while making the filling.

2 Melt the butter in a skillet and sauté the onion for 3 minutes. Add the garlic and cremini mushrooms and sauté for 3 minutes. Add the dried mushrooms to the pan with any liquid and the herbs, sherry, and cream. Season with a little salt and pepper and cook gently for 2 minutes.

3 Fold the crêpes into quarters. Open them out like cones and fill with some of the mushroom mixture. Arrange in a lightly greased, shallow baking dish and bake in a preheated oven at 400°F for 15 minutes. Serve on a bed of lightly wilted spinach or other greens.

Serves 4
Preparation time: **20 minutes, plus crêpe-making time and soaking the mushrooms**
Cooking time: **30 minutes**

buckwheat crêpes with smoked salmon

⅓ cup snipped chives

1¼ cups thick sour cream or crème fraîche

oil or butter, for greasing pan

1 quantity Buckwheat Crêpe batter (*see page* **14**)

12 ounces smoked salmon

salt and pepper

To garnish:

chives

lime wedges

1 Mix together the snipped chives, sour cream or crème fraîche, and a little salt and pepper and set aside.

2 Heat a little oil or butter in a 6-inch crêpe pan until it starts to smoke. Pour in a little batter, tilting the pan until the base is coated with a thin layer. (If you don't have a very small pan use a larger one but only let the batter spread to a diameter of about 6 inches.) Cook for about 1–2 minutes until the underside is golden.

3 Flip the crêpe with an offset spatula and cook for a further 30–45 seconds until golden on the second side. Slide the crêpe out of the pan and make the rest, greasing the pan as necessary.

4 To serve, arrange a little smoked salmon on each crêpe. Place a spoonful of the cream mixture on the salmon and fold over the crêpe to sandwich the filling. Allow 2 or 3 crêpes for each person and garnish them with chives and lime wedges.

Serves 4
Preparation time: **15 minutes**
Cooking time: **15–25 minutes**

shrimp crêpes with dill and sour cream

8 Basic Crêpes (*see page* 12)

¼ **cup butter**

2 **fennel bulbs, trimmed and sliced**

¼ **cup all-purpose flour**

1¼ **cups milk**

⅔ **cup sour cream**

12 **ounces cooked, peeled shrimp,
drained thoroughly**

⅓ **cup roughly chopped dill**

½ **cup grated Parmesan cheese**

salt and pepper

1 Make the crêpes and set them aside while making the filling.

2 Melt the butter in a saucepan and sauté the fennel slices gently for 5 minutes or until soft. Transfer the fennel to a bowl with a slotted spoon. Add the flour to the pan and cook, stirring, for 1 minute. Gradually whisk in the milk and bring to a boil, whisking until thickened. Remove the pan from the heat, stir in the sour cream, and season with salt and pepper to taste.

3 Add the shrimp, dill, and ¾ cup of the sauce to the fennel and mix together. Spoon the filling over the crêpes and roll them up.

4 Put the crêpes in a lightly greased, shallow baking dish and spoon the remaining sauce down the center of the crêpes. Sprinkle with the cheese and bake in a preheated oven at 375°F for 25 minutes or until the sauce is bubbling and lightly golden.

Serves 4
Preparation time: **10 minutes, plus
crêpe-making time**
Cooking time: **40 minutes**

crab crêpe rolls

1 quantity Basic Crêpes
(*see page* 12)

2 tablespoons oil, plus more
for frying

1 bunch of scallions, sliced

2 cups finely shredded white
cabbage

1-inch piece fresh ginger, grated

10 ounces crabmeat

1 teaspoon cornstarch

½ cup dry sherry

2 tablespoons Thai fish sauce

1 egg, beaten

salt and pepper

ready-made sweet chili dipping
sauce, to serve (optional)

These little Asian-style crêpes make an unusual appetizer. They should be no more than 6 inches in diameter. Ideally, you should use a small crêpe pan or skillet, but you could use a larger pan provided you limit the size of the crêpes.

1 Make the crêpes and set them aside while making the filling.

2 Heat the oil in a sauté pan and sauté the scallions and cabbage for 3 minutes. Transfer the mixture to a bowl and stir in the ginger and crabmeat. Mix the cornstarch with the sherry and fish sauce and add to the bowl with a little salt and pepper.

3 Generously brush the edges of a crêpe with beaten egg then pile a tablespoon of the filling in the center. Fold the sides over the filling then roll up the crêpe. Repeat with the remaining crêpes and filling.

4 Heat 2 inches of oil in large pan until a piece of bread sizzles on the surface. Cook the crêpes, a few at a time, for about 1 minute or until golden brown. Drain on paper towels and serve with chili dipping sauce, if desired.

Serves 4
Preparation time: **20 minutes, plus
    crêpe-making time**
Cooking time: **20 minutes**

turkey, tarragon, and mustard crêpes

8 Basic Crêpes (*see page* 12)

¼ **cup butter**

1 **onion, chopped**

2 **garlic cloves, minced**

12 **ounces turkey breast, diced**

2 **tablespoons Dijon mustard**

¼ **cup roughly chopped tarragon**

¾ **cup cooked baby fava beans or English peas**

⅔ **cup crème fraîche**

½ **cup sharp Cheddar cheese, finely grated**

salt and pepper

1 Make the crêpes and set them aside while making the filling.

2 Melt 2 tablespoons of the butter in a sauté pan. Add the onion and sauté gently for 3 minutes. Add the garlic and turkey and sauté for 10 minutes until the turkey is cooked through. Remove the pan from the heat and stir in the mustard, tarragon, fava beans or peas, and crème fraîche and season with salt and pepper.

3 Spoon some of the filling down the center of each crêpe and roll them up. Place them in a lightly greased, shallow baking dish. Melt the remaining butter and spoon it over the crêpes. Sprinkle them with the cheese and cover the dish with foil.

4 Bake the dish in a preheated oven at 400°F for 15–20 minutes until the crêpes are hot.

Serves 4
Preparation time: **10 minutes, plus crêpe-making time**
Cooking time: **35 minutes**

bacon, avocado, and sour cream crêpes

8 Basic Crêpes (*see page* 12)

8 ounces sliced bacon

2 avocados

1¼ cups sour cream

1 garlic clove, crushed

¼ cup snipped chives

½ teaspoon mild chili powder

oil, for greasing baking dish

1 cup finely grated Cheddar cheese

salt and pepper

1 Make the crêpes and set them aside while making the filling.

2 Cook the bacon in a heavy-based pan until crisp. Leave it to cool slightly then cut it into small pieces. Halve, pit, and peel the avocados and slice them thinly. Combine with the bacon. Mix the sour cream with the garlic, chives, chili and salt and pepper. Stir into the bacon and avocado mixture.

3 Divide the mixture among the crêpes, spreading it thinly to within ½ inch of the edge. Roll up the crêpes and place them in a lightly greased, shallow baking dish.

4 Sprinkle the crêpes with the cheese and bake in a preheated oven at 375°F for about 20 minutes until the cheese has melted.

Serves 4
Preparation time: **15 minutes, plus crêpe-making time**
Cooking time: **30 minutes**

ham and gruyère crêpes

1 quantity Basic Crêpes
(*see page* **12**)

1 quantity Béchamel Sauce
(*see page* **20**)

½ cup grated Gruyère cheese

10 ounces ham, sliced

salt and pepper

1 Make the crêpes and allow to cool while making the filling.

2 Make the sauce, remove the pan from the heat and beat in the grated cheese. Season with salt and pepper and leave the sauce to cool.

3 Divide the ham and the cheese sauce among the crêpes, then roll them up and arrange them in a lightly greased, shallow baking dish. Bake in a preheated oven at 400°F for 15 minutes. Serve immediately.

Serves 4
Preparation time: **10 minutes, plus crêpe-making time and making the Béchamel sauce**
Cooking time: **20 minutes**

alsace sausage crêpes

1 quantity Basic Crêpe batter
(*see page* **12**)

8–12 ounces smoked pork sausage, thinly sliced

1½ cups Gruyère cheese, grated

To garnish:

¼ cup chopped parsley

1 shallot, finely chopped

1 garlic clove, minced

1 Lightly grease an 8-inch crêpe pan and heat until very hot. Pour in enough batter to make a very thin crêpe, tilting the pan to ensure an even thickness. When the edges begin to brown, cover the crêpe with some sausage slices and sprinkle with a little cheese.

2 Place under a preheated broiler until the cheese melts. Slide the unfolded crêpe onto a warm ovenproof platter and keep it hot in a preheated oven at 325°F while preparing the remaining crêpes.

3 To serve, mix together the parsley, shallot, and garlic and sprinkle over the crêpes.

Serves 6
Preparation time: **5–10 minutes, plus making the crêpe batter**
Cooking time: **15–25 minutes**

sweet jam crêpes
with crème anglaise

8 Sweet Crêpes (*see page* 15)

1 cup strawberry or raspberry jam

¼ cup lemon juice

superfine sugar, for sprinkling

Crème anglaise:

3 egg yolks

¼ cup superfine sugar

1 teaspoon cornstarch

1 teaspoon vanilla extract

1¼ cups milk

This is a simple and delicious dessert recipe. Crème anglaise is also known as custard cream and vanilla custard; it's a versatile accompaniment which can also be served with fruit, soufflés, and pies.

1 Make the crêpes and set them aside while making the filling.

2 Melt the jam in a small saucepan with the lemon juice. Spread a little of the mixture over each crêpe. Fold them in half, then in half again, and arrange, overlapping, in a lightly greased, shallow baking dish. Bake in a preheated oven at 350°F for about 15 minutes until heated through.

3 Meanwhile, make the crème anglaise. Beat the egg yolks in a bowl with the sugar, cornstarch, vanilla extract, and a little of the milk.

4 Bring the remaining milk to a boil in a heavy-based saucepan. Pour the hot milk over the egg yolk mixture, stirring, and then pour it back into the pan. Cook over a very gentle heat, stirring until the crème anglaise thickens. (Do not boil or the mixture might curdle.) Sprinkle the crêpes with superfine sugar and serve with the crème anglaise.

Serves 4
Preparation time: **10 minutes, plus crêpe-making time**
Cooking time: **20 minutes**

apple and golden raisin crêpes

8 Sweet Crêpes (*see page* 15)

5 Granny Smith apples or similar tart apples

3 tablespoons sweet butter

½ cup sliced almonds

⅓ cup light brown sugar

¼ cup lemon juice

½ cup golden raisins

1 teaspoon apple pie spice

⅓ cup water

whipped cream or vanilla ice cream, to serve

1 Make the crêpes and keep them warm while making the filling. Meanwhile, peel, core, and thinly slice the apples.

2 Melt the butter in a sauté pan and sauté the almonds for 1–2 minutes until golden. Lift them out with a slotted spoon. Add the apples to the pan and sauté for 5 minutes until softened.

3 Add the sugar and cook for 1 minute until dissolved. Stir in the lemon juice, golden raisins, apple pie spice, and water. Cook for 1 minute until bubbling.

4 Using the slotted spoon, place a little of the filling down the center of each crêpe and roll it up. Transfer the crêpes to warm dessert plates and drizzle with the syrup remaining in the pan. Scatter with the almonds and serve with whipped cream or ice cream.

Serves 4
Preparation time: **15 minutes, plus crêpe-making time**
Cooking time: **15 minutes**

buckwheat crêpes with caramelized figs, goat cheese, and honey

8 Buckwheat Crêpes (*see page* 14)

4 ripe figs

¼ **cup orange juice**

¼ **cup superfine sugar**

finely grated zest of 1 orange

4 ounces soft, rindless goat cheese

¾ **cup chestnut or orange blossom honey**

This unusual combination of ingredients adds up to a special finale for a summer meal.

1 Make the crêpes and set them aside while making the toppings.

2 Make two deep cuts crosswise through each fig, leaving the figs intact at the base, and place them in a lightly greased, shallow baking dish. Open the tops out slightly and sprinkle with the orange juice and 2 tablespoons of the sugar. Bake in a preheated oven at 425°F for 15 minutes or until lightly caramelized.

3 While the figs are cooking, wrap the crêpes in foil and put them in the oven for 10 minutes to heat through.

4 Beat the goat cheese with the orange zest and the remaining sugar until soft. Crumple a crêpe on a warm dessert plate and top with a second crumpled crêpe. Repeat with the remaining crêpes on the other dessert plates. Top each one with a spoonful of the goat cheese and a fig.

5 Stir the honey into the juices left in the fig dish and drizzle over the crêpes.

Serves 4
Preparation time: **10 minutes, plus crêpe-making time**
Cooking time: **15 minutes**

crêpes suzette

**1 quantity Basic Crêpes
(*see page* 12)**

¼ cup butter

¼ cup superfine sugar

grated zest and juice of 2 oranges

¼ cup Grand Marnier

¼ cup brandy

crème fraîche, to serve

1 Make the crêpes and set them aside while making the sauce.

2 To make the sauce, melt the butter in a skillet, add the sugar, orange zest and juice, and heat until bubbling. Dip each crêpe into the sauce, fold it into quarters and place on a warm serving platter.

3 Add the Grand Marnier and brandy to the pan; heat gently, then ignite. Pour the flaming liquid over the crêpes and serve immediately with crème fraîche.

Serves 4
Preparation time: **10 minutes, plus crêpe-making time**
Cooking time: **10 minutes**

rum and banana crêpes

**1 quantity Sweet Crêpes
(*see page* 15)**

4 bananas

2 teaspoons lemon juice

**¼ cup superfine sugar, plus extra
for serving**

2 teaspoons cornstarch

⅔ cup rum

1 Make the crêpes and keep them warm while making the filling.

2 Mash the bananas with the lemon juice and sugar. Blend the cornstarch with the rum in a saucepan. Heat, stirring, until the mixture thickens. Stir in the bananas and cook for 1 minute.

3 Divide the banana mixture between the crêpes. Roll them up and arrange on a warm serving platter and dust with sugar. Serve at once.

Serves 4
Preparation time: **10 minutes, plus crêpe-making time**
Cooking time: **5 minutes**

blueberry crêpes

1 quantity Basic Crêpes (*see page* 12)

2 cups fresh blueberries or canned blueberries in natural juice, drained

¼ cup superfine sugar

1 cup water

¼ cup sweet butter

¼ cup crème de cassis

¼ cup brandy

1 Make the crêpes and set them aside while making the filling.

2 Put the blueberries in a heavy-based saucepan and add the sugar and water. Cook over a low heat until the sugar dissolves, then increase the heat slightly and cook, stirring occasionally, until the blueberries are soft. Strain the blueberries through a fine sieve, pressing them lightly with the back of a spoon to extract all the juice. Discard the contents of the sieve.

3 Melt the butter in a large heavy-based frying pan. One by one, coat the crêpes with the butter, folding them in half then in half again as they are coated and pushing them to the side of the pan. Pour the blueberry juice into the frying pan and gently spoon it over the crêpes until they are covered.

4 Mix together the crème de cassis and brandy and warm gently. Pour over the crêpes and ignite carefully. Once the flames die down, transfer the contents of the pan to warm dessert plates and serve immediately.

Serves 4
Preparation time: **10 minutes, plus crêpe-making time**
Cooking time: **30 minutes**

strawberry crêpes

1 quantity Sweet Crêpes
(*see page* 15)

1½ cups strawberries, sliced

½ cup confectioner's sugar, sifted

½ cup brandy

2 tablespoons butter

Oranges have a natural affinity with strawberries, so an orange ice cream or sorbet would go well with these crêpes.

1 Make the crêpes and set them aside while making the filling.

2 To make the filling, mix the strawberries, sugar, and 2 tablespoons of the brandy. Cover and chill until it is needed.

3 Divide the strawberry mixture among the crêpes. Fold them into quarters and arrange in a lightly greased, shallow baking dish. Dot with butter and bake in a preheated oven at 400°F for 10 minutes. Warm the remaining brandy, pour it over the crêpes, set it alight, and serve.

Serves 4
Preparation time: **10 minutes, plus crêpe-making time**
Cooking time: **10 minutes**

sweet cheese crêpes with sour cherry compôte

8 Sweet Crêpes (*see page* 15)

1¼ cups cream cheese

2 teaspoons vanilla extract

2 tablespoons superfine sugar

finely grated zest of 1 orange

1 egg, lightly beaten

1 egg yolk

confectioner's sugar, for dusting

Compôte:

⅓ cup superfine sugar

⅔ cup water

1 cinnamon stick, halved

2 cups pitted fresh sour cherries

1 teaspoon cornstarch

1 Make the crêpes and allow them to cool while making the filling.

2 Beat together the cream cheese, vanilla extract, and sugar until softened. Add the orange zest, egg, and egg yolk and beat until smooth. Place a spoonful in the center of each crêpe. Fold over two sides to enclose the filling, then fold over the other two sides to make little parcels.

3 Arrange the crêpes in a lightly greased, shallow baking dish and bake in a preheated oven at 350°F for 10 minutes.

4 Meanwhile, make the cherry compôte. Put the sugar in a saucepan with the water and heat until the sugar dissolves. Add the cinnamon and cherries and cook gently for 10 minutes or until the cherries have softened but still hold their shape. Blend the cornstarch with a little water and add to the pan. Heat gently, stirring, until the compôte thickens slightly.

5 Transfer the crêpes to dessert plates and dust with confectioner's sugar. Serve with the compôte spooned around them.

Serves 4
Preparation time: **20 minutes, plus crêpe-making time**
Cooking time: **15 minutes**

pineapple and walnut crêpes

8 Sweet Crêpes (*see page* 15)

1 small ripe pineapple

3 oranges

¼ cup walnuts, chopped

½ teaspoon cornstarch

⅔ cup freshly squeezed orange juice

⅓ cup kirsch

superfine sugar, for dusting

lightly whipped cream, to serve

1 Make the crêpes and set aside while making the filling.

2 Cut the skin away from the pineapple. Discard the core and cut the flesh into small pieces. Remove the rind from the oranges. Working over a bowl to catch the juices, cut out the segments from between the membranes. Mix the orange segments with the pineapple and walnuts.

3 Blend the cornstarch with a little of the orange juice in a small saucepan. Add the remaining juice and any orange juice left in the bowl. Cook gently, stirring until thickened. Stir in the kirsch, then stir ½ cup of the sauce into the fruit mixture.

4 Fold a crêpe in half, then in half again. Open it out to form a cone and fill with a little of the fruit mixture. Place in a lightly greased, shallow baking dish and repeat with the remaining crêpes. Dust with a little superfine sugar and bake in a preheated oven at 400°F for 10–15 minutes until heated through.

5 Transfer the crêpes to warm dessert plates. Spoon the remaining sauce over the crêpes and serve with lightly whipped cream.

Serves 4
Preparation time: **20 minutes, plus crêpe-making time**
Cooking time: **15–20 minutes**

apricot and hazelnut crêpes

8 Sweet Crêpes (*see page* 15)

10 fresh apricots, about 1 pound

¼ cup lemon juice

¼ cup light brown sugar, plus more for sprinkling

1 teaspoon ground cinnamon

½ cup hazelnuts, chopped

crème fraîche or yogurt, to serve

1 Make the crêpes and set them aside while making the filling.

2 Halve, pit, and thinly slice the apricots. Toss in a bowl with the lemon juice. Spread the sliced apricots over the crêpes and sprinkle with the sugar, cinnamon, and hazelnuts. Roll up the crêpes and arrange in a lightly greased, shallow baking dish.

3 Sprinkle the crêpes with a little more sugar and bake in a preheated oven at 375°F for 15 minutes. Serve the crêpes warm with crème fraîche or yogurt.

Serves 4
Preparation time: **15 minutes, plus crêpe-making time**
Cooking time: **15 minutes**

melba crêpes

8 Sweet Crêpes (*see page* 15)

¼ cup lemon juice

½ cup confectioner's sugar

4 ripe peaches, peeled, pitted, and sliced

1¼ cups raspberries

crème fraîche and honey, to serve

1 Make the crêpes. Drizzle 4 of them with the lemon juice and sprinkle with about ⅓ cup of the confectioner's sugar. Cover each crêpe with a second one and then scrunch them up into rounds about 6 inches in diameter. Transfer to a lightly greased baking sheet and bake in a preheated oven at 400°F for 6–8 minutes until hot.

2 Transfer the crêpes to warm dessert plates. Scatter the peach slices and raspberries over them and top with crème fraîche and honey. Dust with the remaining sugar and serve immediately.

Serves 4
Preparation time: **10 minutes, plus crêpe-making time**
Cooking time: **6–8 minutes**

lemon soufflé crêpes

1 quantity Basic Crêpes (*see page* 12)

2 tablespoons butter

¼ cup all-purpose flour

1¼ cups milk

2 tablespoons superfine sugar

grated zest and juice of 1 lemon

2 eggs, separated, plus 1 extra egg white

¼ cup confectioner's sugar

1 Make the crêpes and set aside while making the filling.

2 To make the filling, melt the butter in a saucepan, stir in the flour, and cook for 2–3 minutes. Add the milk, sugar, and lemon zest and juice. Bring to a boil, stirring until thickened. Cool slightly, then beat in the egg yolks. Beat the egg whites until stiff and fold them in.

3 Fill and fold the crêpes and arrange them in a lightly greased shallow baking dish. Dust with confectioner's sugar. Bake in a preheated oven at 400°F for 10–15 minutes.

Serves 4
Preparation time: **20 minutes, plus crêpe-making time**
Cooking time: **20–25 minutes**

praline almond crêpes

¼ **cup almonds, ground in a food processor and toasted**

1 teaspoon almond extract

½ **cup milk**

1 quantity Basic Crêpe batter (*see page* 12)

oil or butter, for greasing pan

⅓ **cup superfine sugar**

½ **cup water**

¾ **cup whole blanched almonds**

¾ **cup sweet butter, softened**

superfine sugar, for sprinkling

whipped cream or ice cream, to serve (optional)

1 Beat the ground almonds, almond extract, and milk into the basic batter and cook the crêpes following the instructions on page 12.

2 Brush a small baking sheet with oil. To make the filling, put the sugar in a small heavy-based saucepan with the water. Heat gently, stirring until the sugar dissolves completely, then bring the syrup to a boil and cook, tilting the pan occasionally, until it turns a golden caramel. Immediately remove the pan from the heat, stir in the blanched almonds and pour out onto the baking sheet. Leave until it hardens.

3 Place the almond brittle in a sturdy plastic bag and beat with a rolling pin to break it into small pieces. Transfer to a food processor and grind until finely chopped.

4 Beat the butter in a bowl until softened, then stir in the chopped brittle. Spread this praline mixture over the crêpes and roll them up. Arrange in a lightly greased, shallow baking dish and sprinkle with a little extra sugar. Bake in a preheated oven at 375°F for 10 minutes until warmed through. Serve warm with whipped cream or ice cream, if desired.

Serves 6
Preparation time: **20 minutes**
Cooking time: **35 minutes**

crêpes with hazelnut sauce

1 quantity Basic Crêpe batter
(*see page* 12)

oil or butter, for greasing pan

Filling:

1½ cups hazelnuts, ground in a food
processor

1¼ cups heavy or whipping cream

¾ cup confectioner's sugar

These sweet and satisfying crêpes have a rich and nutty flavor, perfect for fall and winter dinner parties.

1 Make the batter, lightly grease a 10-inch crêpe pan or skillet, and cook 4 large crêpes, following the instructions on page 12. Keep the crêpes warm while you make the filling.

2 To make the filling, mix together half of the hazelnuts, ½ cup of the cream, and half of the confectioner's sugar. Divide the filling among the crêpes and roll them up. Place on a warm serving platter.

3 Gently heat the remaining hazelnuts, cream, and confectioner's sugar in a saucepan and pour over the crêpes.

Makes 4
Preparation time: **15 minutes**
Cooking time: **15 minutes**

crêpes with chestnut cream and amaretto

1 quantity Basic Crêpes
(*see page* 12)

Chestnut cream:

**1 cup unsweetened
chestnut purée**

**grated zest of 1 orange, plus extra
to decorate**

¼ cup Amaretto di Saronno

¼ cup sugar

1¼ cups whipping cream

Chestnut syrup:

1¼ cups maple syrup

**⅔ cup finely chopped, cooked
chestnuts**

¼ cup Amaretto di Saronno

Any liqueur may be used in this recipe; try experimenting with Cointreau, Drambuie, or brandy.

1 Make the crêpes and keep them warm while making the filling.

2 To make the chestnut cream, put the chestnut purée in a large bowl with the orange zest, Amaretto, and sugar and mix together. In another bowl, whip the cream until it forms soft peaks. Fold the cream into the chestnut mixture and refrigerate until needed.

3 To make the chestnut syrup, heat the maple syrup and chopped chestnuts in a saucepan, bring to a boil and stir in the Amaretto.

4 Fill the crêpes with the chestnut cream, roll them up, and arrange on individual plates or on a warm serving platter. Drizzle the heated syrup over the crêpes and serve immediately, decorated with grated orange zest.

Serves 4
Preparation time: **15 minutes, plus
crêpe-making time**
Cooking time: **10 minutes**

chocolate and banana crêpe torte

¼ cup hazelnuts or almonds, ground in a food processor and toasted

1 teaspoon almond extract

½ cup milk

1 quantity Sweet Crêpe batter (*see page* 15)

oil or butter, for greasing pan

1½ cups chocolate and hazelnut spread

½ cup heavy or whipping cream

5 large bananas

¼ cup lemon juice

confectioner's sugar, for sprinkling

¼ cup hazelnuts, toasted and roughly chopped

whipped cream, to serve (optional)

Although delicious served at room temperature, this dessert can also be warmed through before serving. Assemble it on a baking sheet instead of a plate and warm in a preheated oven at 400°F for 10 minutes.

1 Beat the ground nuts, almond extract, and milk into the crêpe batter and cook the crêpes following the instructions on page 15. Set the crêpes aside while making the filling

2 Put the chocolate spread in a small pan with the cream and heat gently until slightly softened but not liquid. Slice the bananas as thinly as possible and toss in the lemon juice.

3 Place a crêpe on a flat plate and spread with a little of the chocolate spread. Cover with a thin layer of banana slices. Arrange another crêpe on top. Continue layering the ingredients, finishing with a crêpe. Sprinkle with confectioner's sugar and scatter with toasted hazelnuts. Serve cut into wedges with whipped cream, if desired.

Serves 6
Preparation time: **15 minutes, plus making the crêpe batter**
Cooking time: **25 minutes**

baked crêpes with glossy chocolate sauce

1 quantity Basic Crêpes
(*see page* 12)

1 cup ricotta cheese

⅓ cup superfine sugar

1 cup fresh or frozen
blueberries, thawed

¾ cup white chocolate chips

½ cup heavy or whipping cream

Glossy chocolate sauce:

½ cup superfine sugar

⅓ cup water

7 squares semisweet or
bittersweet chocolate

2 tablespoons unsalted butter

Use a chocolate with a high cocoa butter content to make a really rich sauce.

1 Make the crêpes and set them aside while making the filling.

2 To make the filling, mix together the ricotta, sugar, blueberries, white chocolate chips, and cream.

3 Thinly spread the filling over the crêpes then fold them into quarters and arrange in a lightly greased, shallow baking dish. Cook in a preheated oven at 375°F for 8–10 minutes until the filling is warmed through.

4 Meanwhile, make the sauce. Heat the superfine sugar and water in a small heavy-based saucepan until the sugar dissolves. Bring the syrup to a boil and boil rapidly for 1 minute. Remove the pan from the heat and add the chocolate. Leave until it melts, then stir in the butter to make a smooth, glossy sauce. Serve hot, with the crêpes.

Serves 4
Preparation time: **20 minutes, plus crêpe-making time**
Cooking time: **8–10 minutes**

hot chocolate crêpes with spiced ricotta and raisins

1 quantity Chocolate Crêpes
(*see page* 16)

superfine sugar, for dusting

1 quantity Glossy Chocolate Sauce
(*see page* 62)

lightly whipped cream, to serve
(optional)

Filling:

1 piece of crystallized ginger
(about ½ ounce), finely chopped

¼ cup superfine sugar

1 cup ricotta cheese

½ cup raisins

1 cup finely chopped
white chocolate

⅓ cup heavy or whipping cream

1 Make the crêpes and set them aside while making the filling.

2 To make the filling, mix the ginger in a bowl with the sugar, ricotta, raisins, white chocolate, and cream. Place spoonfuls of the filling in the center of the crêpes and fold them into quarters, enclosing the filling.

3 Place the crêpes in a lightly greased, shallow baking dish and dust with sugar. Bake in a preheated oven at 400°F for 10 minutes until heated through. Serve hot with the glossy chocolate sauce and cream, if desired.

Serves 4
Preparation time: **20 minutes, plus crêpe-making time**
Cooking time: **10 minutes**

index